THIS BOOK BELONGS TO

Whether you have received this book as a gift or bought it for your own amusement, we hope that you enjoy the bathroom themed puzzles and jokes and get one for your best friend because laughter is what makes life fun and shared laughter is even better.

CORRECT USE OF THE TOILET BRUSH

QUITE WRONG   **MISGUIDED**

ERRONEOUS   **CORRECT**

SMELLS

```
I  T  M  Y  I  T  Q  D  B  F  H  I  C  U  Z
F  N  S  L  T  T  Y  K  I  T  R  T  X  Z  I
V  J  K  F  U  S  T  Y  W  C  W  E  S  B  J
S  N  Q  O  C  N  W  C  T  S  N  K  E  R  Q
T  H  P  G  L  A  E  O  P  S  R  A  N  K  H
I  H  W  H  N  I  M  N  R  P  U  T  R  I  D
N  S  U  O  R  O  D  O  A  F  V  M  U  L  R
K  D  E  B  I  V  P  L  R  G  O  M  J  B  J
Y  W  H  I  F  F  W  I  K  A  F  E  T  I  D
H  L  R  U  O  D  O  L  A  M  U  P  T  A  L
A  C  L  P  J  I  V  B  S  E  N  H  P  I  D
H  Y  N  E  I  B  N  A  S  Y  K  I  R  P  D
Z  A  F  E  M  V  N  T  D  L  Y  T  F  R  U
D  T  O  T  T  S  T  R  O  N  G  I  D  F  S
T  B  U  Y  V  S  W  Q  T  N  E  C  S  W  Y
```

AROMA	MEPHITIC	RANK
FETID	MUSTY	REEK
FOETID	NIFFY	SCENT
FROWSTY	ODOROUS	SMELLY
FUNKY	OLID	STENCH
FUSTY	PONG	STINKY
GAMEY	PUTRID	STRONG
MALODOUR	RANCID	WHIFF

The person who said 'Laughter is the best medicine' clearly never had diahorrea!

Bathroom Riddles

What gets wetter the more it dries?

What word is the same word when viewed backwards and upside down? Hint: you need a lot of water

What is full of holes but can still hold water?

You fill up the bathtub with water. You have a teaspoon, a tablespoon, and a fork. What is the fastest way to empty the bathtub?

Answers: 1) a towel 2) swims 3) a sponge 4) pull the plug

Fill In The Words

5 letters
AMBER
BLOOM
CHICK
GLORY
IVORY
NOVEL
SCENE
SWISS
TRIBE
UMIAK UN
ITE
USHER

6 letters
ACCESS
ARARAT
ELEVEN
EMBLEM
MIRROR
MOHAWK
SCALES
SNOOZE

7 letters
AGELESS
AMATEUR
AMIABLE
ANDORRA
ASH TREE
BALANCE
CLOTHES
REPAINT
DURANGO
ESQUIRE
PANCAKE
PRECISE

7 letters
PROTECT
QUETZAL
ROTATED
SHELTER
STETSON
TOURNEY

11 letters
LIFE SCIENCE
NETHERLANDS
SIGHTSEEING
SOLAR ENERGY

9 letters
AGREEMENT
MICROCOSM
NEWSPAPER
REYKJAVIK
SCIENTIST
SOYA BEANS
SUBMARINE
THOUSANDS

Bathroom Quiz

1) What is the most popular thing to do whilst using the toilet?

a) use a mobile phone

b) Sing loudly because the door lock is broken

c) Calculate if the remaining toilet paper will be enough for your needs

2) How many mobile phones are dropped down the pan every year?

a) 5 million

b) 7 million

c) 9 million

3) What do the majority people do with their toilet paper before using it?
a) crumple it up
b) fold it neatly
c) make an origami bird

4) What percentage of house guest look in other people's bathroom cabinets ?
a) 30%
b) 50%
c) 70%

5) The factory machinery that makes toilet brushes also makes?
a) Toothbrushes
b) Washing up brushes
c) Artificial Christmas Trees

Characterize your poop

Characterize your poop

Q: Why do ducks have feathers?
A: To cover their butt quacks!

Q: Why is a toilet a good place to take a nap?
A: Because it's in the restroom!

Q: What do you get if you mix holy water and castor oil?
A: A religious movement!

Q: Want to hear a poop gag?
A: No thanks – too corny!

Q: What did one fly say to another?
A: Is this stool taken?!

Bathroom Report

Name:	Date:

Time:

Reason for visit:

Cleanliness ☆☆☆☆☆
Ambiance ☆☆☆☆☆
Flush ☆☆☆☆☆
Toilet Paper ☆☆☆☆☆
Soundproofing ☆☆☆☆☆

Whilst here, did you:

○ Text someone
○ Make a phone call
○ Check social media
○ Take a selfie
○ Snoop in the cabinet

○ Talk to yourself
○ Brush your hair
○ Check out your butt in mirror
○ Stay in longer than required
○ Someone knocked on the door

Would Poop Here Again ☆☆☆☆☆
Highly Commended for a Poop ☆☆☆☆
Couldn't Finish My Business ☆☆☆
Toilet Paper Ran Out ☆☆
Only if Really Really Desperate ☆

Final Thoughts:

Please Don't Flush

Paper Towels

Nappies

Gum

Your phone

A Photo Of Your Ex

Hopes & Dreams

Junk Mail

Goldfish

Wipes

Love Letters

Girly Things

Kittens

Odd Socks

The Head Of Your Enemy

Friendships

Solution at the back of the book

Bathology

Sitting in a hot bath and pouring a bottle of cold sparkling water over yourself.
Have you tried this? ☐ Yes ☐ No, but I'd like to

Bathpetite

You want to use the bathroom but when you see the unhygienic state it is in, you change your mind
Write about an occasion this happened to you...

_____

_____

_____

_____

Solve these clues.
All answers contain poo

1) Not enough money to spend a penny (4) ....

2) Unravel (7) ....

3) Share a ride (7) ....
   (Never fart in an enclosed space!)

4) Funny imitation of Trump? (7) ....

5) A trail left by an animal (5) ....

6) Russian weight equal to 36 pounds (4)...................

7) Water going down the pan (9)..............................

8) Wading bird (9) ....

9) The rear of a ship (5) ....

10) Spear for catching large fish (7) ....

Answers at the back of the book

BATHROOMS

```
W  S  H  A  M  P  O  O  Y  S  L  E  U  B  M
J  I  N  Q  O  F  B  M  I  R  R  O  R  K  W
A  N  K  T  Q  Z  W  A  M  T  D  C  F  G  A
M  K  S  C  O  N  D  I  T  I  O  N  E  R  S
T  M  O  K  O  I  A  B  X  H  O  W  U  A  H
O  E  A  H  T  L  L  M  U  A  R  M  E  A  C
I  D  P  G  S  A  R  E  S  T  I  O  T  L  L
L  I  W  I  A  U  M  O  T  E  H  Q  B  I  O
E  C  B  T  R  Z  R  H  O  P  U  T  J  E  T
T  I  T  I  E  C  I  B  T  D  A  S  A  O  H
B  N  V  D  F  N  A  N  H  A  M  P  S  B  G
R  E  U  X  K  Z  I  C  E  T  B  Y  E  I  R
U  S  C  A  L  E  S  B  L  J  O  D  V  R  T
S  H  O  W  E  R  P  L  A  N  T  O  W  M  J
H  S  C  I  T  E  M  S  O  C  W  D  T  I  H
```

BATH MAT	MAGAZINE	SOAP
BATHROBE	MEDICINE	TISSUES
BATHTUB	MIRROR	TOILET BRUSH
CABINET	PLANT	TOILET PAPER
CONDITIONER	SCALES	TOOTHBRUSH
COSMETICS	SHAMPOO	TOWEL
DOOR LOCK	SHOWER	WASHCLOTH
LAUNDRY	SINK	

Did you hear about the constipated accountant? He couldn't budget!

Write down as many words as you can. Each word must use the central letter and be at least 3 letters long.

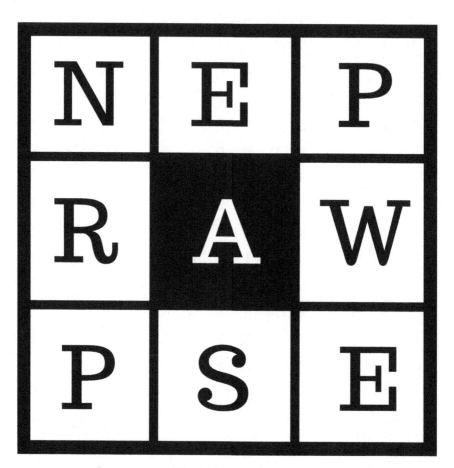

100 words: excellent

80 words: very good

50 words: good

30 words: poor

10 words: crap

Clue for 9 letter word: helpful if you have a toilet paper shortage

CODEBREAKER WORD PUZZLE

The same number represents the same letter. Crack the code and fill the grid. To help you get started some words are already in place.

	1		2		3		4	5	6	7	8	9	5		10		11	
12	10	13	14	8	7	6		15		6		7		7 A	1 P	14 R	4 I	6 L
	1		4		16		5	13	1	1	10	14	17		7		8	
17	13	14	17	6	18	5		7		19		16	4	17	3	19	18	8
	6		4		5	13	14	14	18	7	6		17		4		20	
1	7	4	8	17		8		18		21		1	6	7	17	18	7	13
	14		20	4	7	8	17		14	18	11	13	18		22		14	
20		5		8		22		5		17		1		14		1		4
14	18	8	10	2	8		3	4	11	4	6	4	23	7	17	4	10	8
18		4		7		5 S		20		3		6		4		1		9
18	24	1	18	14	4	25 M	18	8	17	7	6		10	8	6	4	8	18
8		18		18		4 I		4		6		21		21		17		24
	26		5		3	6 L	4	26	26		17	14	10	10	1		17	
25	4	24	17	13	14	18 E		4		1		10		2	19	18	7	17
	20		13		10		10	3	17	7	20	10	8		22		8	
5	13	8	9	10	2	8		7		14		25	18	5	5	7	20	18
	14		18		8	13	7	8	3	18	5		5		4		6	
5	18	8	8	7		17		3		8		5	17	4	3	16	18	14
	5		17		7	5	1	18	3	17	5		5		5		9	

1	2	3	4	5	6	7	8	9	10	11	12	13
14	15	16	17	18	19	20	21	22	23	24	25	26

ANSWER: 1=P, 2=W, 3=C, 4=I, 5=S, 6=L, 7=A, 8=N, 9=D, 10=O, 11=V, 12=J, 13=U, 14=R, 15=Q, 16=K, 17=T, 18=E, 19=H, 20=G, 21=B, 22=Y, 23=Z, 24=X, 25=M, 26=F.

Sit, Relax and Let go

SOLVE THESE ANAGRAMS

All are words for a fixed receptacle into which a person may urinate or defecate, typically consisting of a large bowl connected to a system for flushing away the waste into a sewer.

/// ○ \\\ ○ /// ○ \\\ ○ /// ○ \\\ ○ /// ○ \\\ ○ /// ○ \\\ ○ /// ○ \\\ ○ /// ○ \\\ ○ /// ○ \\\ ○

1) HORNET TEN OH ....
2) FOIL OF CAVE ....
3) WHO BEEPING HIT ....
4) SEA SUE HONK ....
5) ICED LUG ....
6) BOND HER TUX ....
7) LOOPS TOOL ....
8) BOD CHIN ....

/// ○ \\\ ○ /// ○ \\\ ○ /// ○ \\\ ○ /// ○ \\\ ○ /// ○ \\\ ○ /// ○ \\\ ○ /// ○ \\\ ○ /// ○ \\\ ○

CHILDREN ARE LIKE FARTS

Your own are just about tolerable,
but everyone else's are unbearable.

/// ○ \\\ ○ /// ○ \\\ ○ /// ○ \\\ ○ /// ○ \\\ ○ /// ○ \\\ ○ /// ○ \\\ ○ /// ○ \\\ ○ /// ○ \\\ ○

Answers: 1) On The Throne 2) Oval Office 3) Big White Phone 4) Snakehouse 5) Cludgie 6) Thunderbox 7) Stool Pool 8) Chodbin

6	2			4		7		5
			5		9	3	6	4
			6				1	2
			2	5		1	4	
			9		3			8
		9						
9		4		8				
		7				4		
2	8			7			5	3

Toilet paper - what a rip-off!

Having a poo is a number 2
So should a pee be a number 3?

WACKY WORDS

stand I	pleasant CCU
now in here	S T ONE
CCCCCCCCC	EACK

CHESS

MOTHER

ON
RO   AD

Head
Ton 4 Arms
Legs

cover
cop

Bathroom Slang

Answer the call of nature

Syphon the python

Powder my nose

Going to water my horse

Draining the lizard

Point Percy at the Porcelain

Taking a Chinese singing lesson

Visit Uncle Charley

Wash my mongoose

Taking a slash

Pay the water bill

Flush my buffers

Pass water

Splashing the pirate

Make my bladder gladder

Breaking the seal

Steering Stanley to the stainless steel

Bathroom Report

Name:	Date:

Time:	Reason for visit:

Cleanliness ☆☆☆☆☆
Ambiance ☆☆☆☆☆
Flush ☆☆☆☆☆
Toilet Paper ☆☆☆☆☆
Soundproofing ☆☆☆☆☆

Whilst here, did you:

○ Text someone
○ Make a phone call
○ Check social media
○ Take a selfie
○ Snoop in the cabinet

○ Talk to yourself
○ Brush your hair
○ Check out your butt in mirror
○ Stay in longer than required
○ Someone knocked on the door

Would Poop Here Again ☆☆☆☆☆
Highly Commended for a Poop ☆☆☆☆☆
Couldn't Finish My Business ☆☆☆
Toilet Paper Ran Out ☆☆
Only if Really Really Desperate ☆

Final Thoughts:

What Did People Use Before Toilet Paper Was Invented?

Vikings: Sheep's wool

British Posh People: Pages from a book

US: Newsprint and paper catalog pages

Mayans: Corn on the cob husks (rough!)

India: Water and your left hand

Hawaii: Coconut shells (a bit rough!)

French Royalty: Lace

Poor Romans: A sponge soaked in salt water or vinegar on the end of a stick (nasty if you have a cut)

Rich Romans: Wool and Rosewater

Greeks: Clay

Eskimos: moss or snow (bracing!)

Finish the doodle

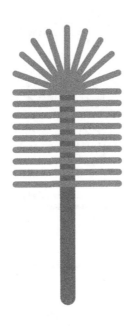

Find the 2 identical Bathroom Keys

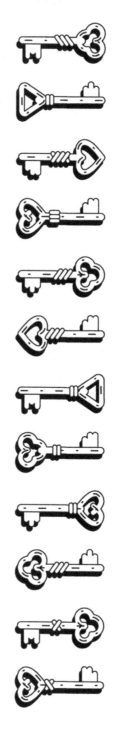

TOILETRIES

```
B  X  P  O  H  A  I  R  D  R  Y  E  R  X  W
H  E  M  E  R  Y  B  O  A  R  D  C  X  Y  L
R  M  N  X  M  H  A  I  R  B  R  U  S  H  U
A  O  P  G  F  Z  T  E  M  U  F  R  E  P  U
C  I  U  J  O  U  H  I  P  B  B  R  V  W  U
F  S  B  T  G  L  B  B  W  B  R  O  Z  A  R
R  T  O  W  S  S  O  L  F  L  A  T  N  E  D
N  U  D  E  P  I  M  C  L  E  G  R  I  A  H
A  R  Y  E  O  H  B  O  O  B  S  E  P  I  W
I  I  L  Z  W  Q  V  M  M  A  K  E  U  P  H
L  Z  O  E  D  K  N  B  D  T  V  S  L  Q  A
F  E  T  R  E  H  S  A  W  H  T  U  O  M  F
I  R  I  S  R  E  P  P  O  R  D  E  Y  E  R
L  O  O  F  A  H  M  A  E  R  C  D  N  A  H
E  A  N  T  I  S  E  P  T  I  C  S  O  A  P
```

ANTISEPTIC   EYEDROPPER   MOUTHWASH
BATH BOMB   HAIR BRUSH   NAIL FILE
BODY LOTION   HAIR DRYER   PERFUME
BUBBLE BATH   HAIR GEL   POWDER
COLOGNE   HAND CREAM   RAZOR
COMB   LOOFAH   SOAP
DENTAL FLOSS   MAKEUP   TWEEZERS
EMERY BOARD   MOISTURIZER   WIPES

May your life be like toilet paper:
long and useful

Write down as many words as you can. Each word must use the central letter and be at least 3 letters long.

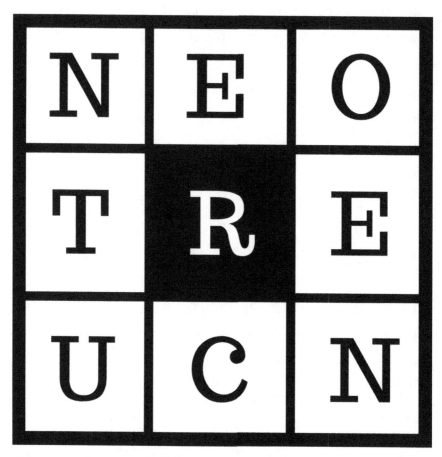

80 words: excellent

60 words: very good

40 words: good

20 words: poor

10 words: your turn to clean the bathroom

Clue for 9 letter word: meeting someone in the restroom

Find 10 differences

Between these two pictures

bathroom

bath . room /ˈbaTHˌroom/ noun

A PLACE FOR INTROVERTS
TO HIDE AT PARTIES

Is that what you're doing right now?

To make a word, take a letter or combination of letters from each toilet paper. Make four words for each puzzle.

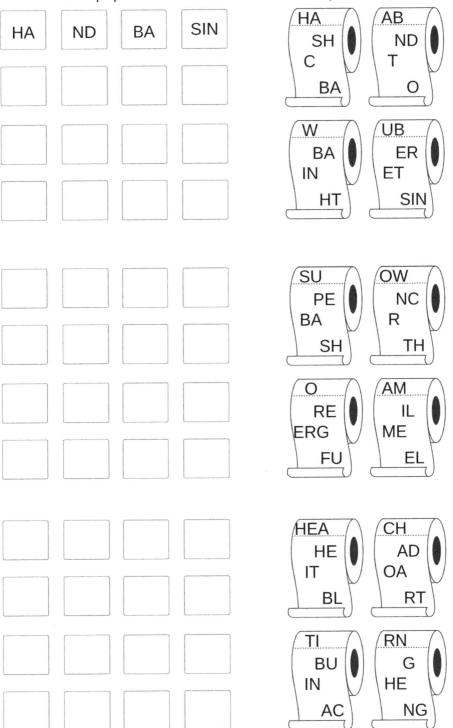

HA	ND	BA	SIN

HA
SH
C
BA

AB
ND
T
O

W
BA
IN
HT

UB
ER
ET
SIN

SU
PE
BA
SH

OW
NC
R
TH

O
RE
ERG
FU

AM
IL
ME
EL

HEA
HE
IT
BL

CH
AD
OA
RT

TI
BU
IN
AC

RN
G
HE
NG

"But I promised the other guys I wouldn't shave."

5	2	6	3	1		8		
	9		6	8				
4								
8		1		2		5		
		3	8		9		4	6
	7				1			
7			1	4				2
	8		7					5
					6	7		3

I ate 4 cans of alphabet spaghetti yesterday and today I had the biggest vowel movement ever!

Bathroom Report

Name:	Date:

Time:

Cleanliness	☆☆☆☆☆
Ambiance	☆☆☆☆☆
Flush	☆☆☆☆☆
Toilet Paper	☆☆☆☆☆
Soundproofing	☆☆☆☆☆

Reason for visit:

Whilst here, did you:

- ◯ Text someone
- ◯ Make a phone call
- ◯ Check social media
- ◯ Take a selfie
- ◯ Snoop in the cabinet
- ◯ Talk to yourself
- ◯ Brush your hair
- ◯ Check out your butt in mirror
- ◯ Stay in longer than required
- ◯ Someone knocked on the door

Would Poop Here Again	☆☆☆☆☆
Highly Commended for a Poop	☆☆☆☆
Couldn't Finish My Business	☆☆☆
Toilet Paper Ran Out	☆☆
Only if Really Really Desperate	☆

Final Thoughts:

LIVE
LAUGH
POOP

How To Make Your Poo Funny Colors

Disclaimer: This is NOT medical advice

Brown: Great news! This is how it should be! You poo is probably brown anyway so if this is your favorite color, you are in luck.

Green: Try eating a lot of leafy green vegetables eg spinach? It's a fun thing to try for St Patricks Day especially if you have Irish heritage.

Yellow: You don't really want poo that is yellow all over but it does look pretty dotted with sweetcorn. Sweetcorn is a lovely bright yellow and also a tasty vegetable.

Black: Easily achieved if your doctor has give you iron tablets. If not, try Oreos. Lots of Oreos.
I know which I prefer...

Pink: Beetroot is your friend if you want pink poo. Remember that you ate the beetroot or you will frighten yourself to death when you spot the glowing pinkness in the pan.

Purple with sparkly bits: no chance unless you are a unicorn.

THE BATHROOM

```
R  W  D  G  G  P  T  H  R  O  N  E  L  P  H
H  L  Z  R  B  L  L  E  T  U  C  E  P  V  W
N  N  P  W  R  R  H  A  O  C  R  X  O  C  A
Q  N  S  E  S  I  A  D  V  A  E  A  W  M  T
E  R  W  S  C  T  E  S  L  A  S  D  D  Y  E
Y  F  M  E  R  N  N  A  C  B  T  E  E  R  R
O  N  H  O  J  E  E  E  C  O  R  O  R  D  C
I  L  X  L  O  O  P  I  G  G  O  N  R  S  L
F  U  A  J  O  R  O  P  N  G  O  D  O  Y  O
Y  Q  M  T  Q  N  K  L  A  E  M  U  O  T  S
F  Y  V  I  R  P  G  A  X  R  V  N  M  L  E
P  I  S  S  O  I  R  D  O  G  C  N  C  K  T
P  N  N  C  P  H  N  I  R  L  V  Y  O  K  A
D  M  Q  I  Z  R  L  E  P  O  C  B  Y  C  B
U  U  M  O  O  R  H  S  A  W  P  Z  R  S  R
```

BOGGER	HEADS	POWDER ROOM
BRASCO	JOHN	PRIVY
CAN	LADIES	RESTROOM
CLOAKROOM	LATRINE	THRONE
CONVENIENCE	LAVATORY	WASHROOM
CRAPPER	LONGDROP	WATER CLOSET
DUNNY	LOO	
GENTS	PISSOIR	

Today was a record!
10 different girls asked me to go out!
I was in the womens bathroom...

Finish the doodle

Fill In The Words

5 letters	6 letters	7 letters	7 letters	9 letters
AMBER	AMULET	ARRANGE	PEN NAME	ALABASTER
CLERK	COLLIE	BAY LEAF	PYRAMID	COWBOY HAT
CLIFF	FOLDED	BEAR CUB	SATSUMA	DECORATED
EAGLE	GYPSUM	CAPTCHA	TRIREME	ESKIMO DOG
EGYPT	LEAGUE	CYCLONE	USELESS	FLAMINGOS
EMPTY	LIGHTS	HIT LIST	VEHICLE	GUARANTEE
NYLON	REPEAT	INSTANT		HYBRID CAR
PSALM	RHYTHM	ISLANDS	**11 letters**	TRADITION
RHYME		JAKARTA	RECTANGULAR	
RULER		KINGDOM	RESPONSIBLE	
STRAW		LIBRARY	SOUTHAMPTON	
STYLE		ODYSSEY	WROUGHT IRON	

A CLEAN BOWL IS OUR GOAL

Quick!! You need the bathroom. Work out which way to get there through this maze of rooms.
Closed doors are locked and cannot be used.

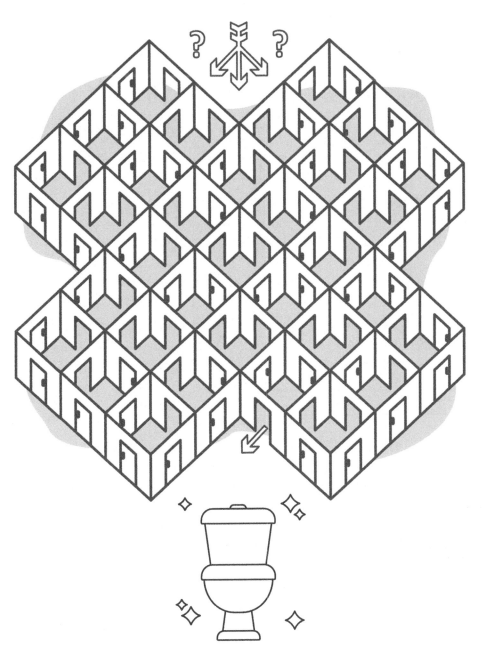

Oh, the relief!

Bathroom Report

| Name: | Date: |

| Time: |

Cleanliness	☆☆☆☆☆
Ambiance	☆☆☆☆☆
Flush	☆☆☆☆☆
Toilet Paper	☆☆☆☆☆
Soundproofing	☆☆☆☆☆

Reason for visit:

Whilst here, did you:

◯ Text someone
◯ Make a phone call
◯ Check social media
◯ Take a selfie
◯ Snoop in the cabinet

◯ Talk to yourself
◯ Brush your hair
◯ Check out your butt in mirror
◯ Stay in longer than required
◯ Someone knocked on the door

Would Poop Here Again	☆☆☆☆☆
Highly Commended for a Poop	☆☆☆☆
Couldn't Finish My Business	☆☆☆
Toilet Paper Ran Out	☆☆
Only if Really Really Desperate	☆

Final Thoughts:

Are you done?

WASH your HANDS

Puzzle Solutions

SMELLS
Puzzle # 1

		Y			D							
			T				I		R			
		F	U	S	T	Y		C		E		
S		O		W		T		N		E		
T		G	L	A		O		S	R	A	N	K
I			N	I	M		R	P	U	T	R	I	D
N	S	U	O	R	O	D	O		F		M	
K				P			R	G	O	M		
Y	W	H	I	F	F			A	F	E	T	I	D
H	L	R	U	O	D	O	L	A	M	U	P	T
	C	L						E	N	H		I
		N	E					Y	K	I			D
		E	M					Y	T	F		
			T	S	T	R	O	N	G	I		F
				S			T	N	E	C	S		Y

BATHROOMS
Puzzle # 2

	S	H	A	M	P	O	O	Y				
	I				B	M	I	R	R	O	R		W
	N	K	T			A		T	D			A
	K	S	C	O	N	D	I	T	I	O	N	E	R	S
T	M	O		O	I		B		H		W	U		H
O	E	A	H	T	L	L		U		R		E	A	C
I	D	P	G	S	A	R	E	S	T		O		L	L
L	I		A	U	M	O	T	E	H		B		O
E	C		T		Z	R	H	O	P	U	T		E	T
T	I			E		I	B	T	D	A	S	A		H
B	N				N		N	H	A		P	S	B
R	E				I		E	T	B		E	I
U	S	C	A	L	E	S	B			O		R	T
S	H	O	W	E	R	P	L	A	N	T	O
H	S	C	I	T	E	M	S	O	C			T

TOILETRIES
Puzzle # 3

			H	A	I	R	D	R	Y	E	R		
	E	M	E	R	Y	B	O	A	R	D		
	M	N		H	A	I	R	B	R	U	S	H
	O		G		T	E	M	U	F	R	E	P
	I		O		H		B					
	S	B	T		L	B		B	R	O	Z	A	R
	T	O	W	S	S	O	L	F	L	A	T	N	E	D
N	U	D	E	P		M	C	L	E	G	R	I	A	H
A	R	Y	E	O		B	O		B	S	E	P	I	W
I	I	L	Z	W		M	M	A	K	E	U	P
L	Z	O	E	D		B		T
F	E	T	R	E	H	S	A	W	H	T	U	O	M
I	R	I	S	R	E	P	P	O	R	D	E	Y	E
L	O	O	F	A	H	M	A	E	R	C	D	N	A	H
E	A	N	T	I	S	E	P	T	I	C	S	O	A	P

THE BATHROOM
Puzzle # 4

				T	H	R	O	N	E			
			B		L	E				P		W
			R		A			R		O		A
	E	S		A	D	V		E		W		T
		C	T		S		A	S		D		E
M		R	N	N	A	C	B	T		E		R
N	H	O	J	E	E	E		O	R	O	R		C
L		L	O	O	P	I	G	G	O		R		L
A		O	R	O	P	N	G	O	D	O	Y	O
	T		N	K	L	A	E	M	U	O		S
Y	V	I	R	P	G	A		R	V	N	M		E
P	I	S	S	O	I	R	D	O		C	N		T
			N	I	R	L		Y	O		
			E		O	C			C		
	M	O	O	R	H	S	A	W	P			

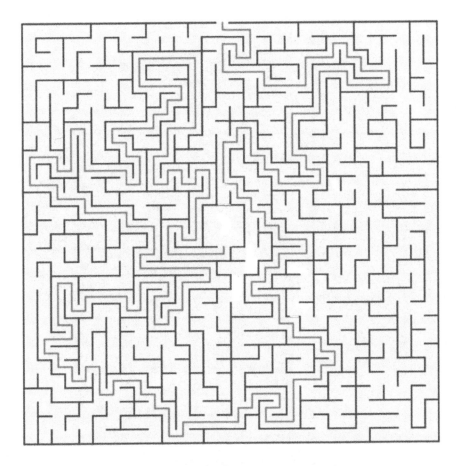

Words containing poo answers

1) poor 2) unspool 3) carpool 4) lampoon
5) spoor 6) pood 7) whirlpool 8) Spoonbill
9) poops 10) harpoon

Answers: HANDBASIN, SHOWER, BATHTUB, CABINET : SUNCREAM, PERFUME,
SHOWER GEL, BATH OIL : HEARTBURN, BLOATING, ITCHING, HEADACHE

Thank you for buying, gifting and reading
'Things To Do While You Poo On The Loo
Book 2'
Book 1 is available and is simply called
'Things To Do While You Poo On The Loo'
by Alex Smart.